Amgueddfa Genedlaethol
National Museum of Wal
1979

CHILDREN WORKING
UNDERGROUND

*This book
belongs to:*

JOHN DAVIES

*This booklet has been written
by R. Meurig Evans of the Schools Service*

ISBN 0 7200 0217 6

Foreword

It is almost beyond understanding that a civilised society should allow children of five years of age to work, not only in factories, but in coalmines and ironworks. Industrial Britain in the late eighteenth and early nineteenth centuries accepted such a labour force as a necessary part of producing much needed raw materials as well as making the finished article.

It is difficult to allocate blame for such inhuman treatment of children, for not only did some managements condone the system but parents too. It must be remembered that it was an age of great contrasts: poverty and wealth, freedom and slavery.

Changes for the better had to come and the government of the day began an investigation into the employment of children. This ultimately resulted in what was to be known as the Commission of Enquiry into the State of Children in Employment. During the early 1840s inspectors visited the whole of industrial Britain taking evidence from employers and employees. Untruths were frequently told during the presentation of evidence: the employees did not want to risk losing their jobs by giving evidence that would discredit the management while the latter wanted, generally speaking, to paint a picture which would be acceptable to the government.

Reading through the reports of the inspectors, however, it is not difficult to realise the terrible existence of whole families and communities whose lives, often short, were committed to working underground.

The government investigated all industries in which children were employed, but this book deals only with mining. Eleven areas only are dealt with in this book and it must be remembered that mining took place in many other parts of Britain. Most of those who speak from these pages are children, although the greater part of the evidence was provided by adults.

There was considerable opposition to the proposal that child labour should be abolished and it was with great difficulty that Lord Shaftesbury's Mines Act was passed in 1842. This made illegal the employment of children under the age of ten years underground. Many years were to pass before complete success was to be achieved and children of all ages could make their way to school instead of to mine or factory.

July 1979

Acknowledgements:
The author wishes to acknowledge the assistance given by Dr. Gerwyn Thomas of the Department of Industry, National Museum of Wales and also Miss Elizabeth Forrest who designed the cover.

The illustrations on pages 24,25,26,27,28,42,43,44,45,46,47 and 57 are from the Museum collection and those on pages 58 and 59 belong to the author.

Other titles in the series:
'Children in the Mines 1840-42'.
'Children in the Iron Industry 1840-42'.
(Both these volumes deal with South Wales only. Welsh language versions of these booklets are also available).

COALFIELDS

TIN, COPPER etc.

East
Scotland

Northumberland

Durham

Yorkshire

South Staffordshire

South Wales

South
Gloucestershire

North
Somerset

South Durham

'The little trapper of eight years lies quiet in bed. It is now between two and three in the morning, and his mother shakes him, and desires him to rise, and tells him that his father has, an hour ago, gone to the pit. He turns on his side, rubs his eyes, and gets up, and comes to the blazing fire, and bread is laid down for him. The fortnight is now well advanced, the money all spent, and butter, bacon and other luxurious accompaniments of bread, are not to be had at breakfast till next pay-day supply the means. He then fills his tin bottle with coffee, and takes a lump of bread, and sets out for the pit, into which he goes down in the cage, and walking along the horse-way for upwards of a mile, he reaches the barrow-way, over which the young men and boys push the trams with the tubs on rails to the flats, where the barrow-way and horse-way meet, and where the tubs are transferred to rolleys or carriages drawn by horses.

'He knows his place of work. It is inside one of the doors called trap-doors, which is in the barrow-way, for the purpose of forcing the stream of air which passes in its long many miled course from the down shaft to the up shaft of the pit; but which door must be opened whenever men or boys, with or without carriages, may wish to pass through. He seats himself in a little hole, about the size of a common fireplace, and with the string in his hand: and all his work is to pull that string when he has to open the door, and when man or boy has passed through, then to allow the door to shut of itself. Here it is his duty to sit, and be attentive, and

7

pull his string promptly as anyone approaches. He may not stir above a dozen of steps with safety from his charge, lest he should be found neglecting his duty, and suffer for the same.'

So wrote the government inspector of one young lad who worked in one of the South Durham mines in 1840. We are not told the name of the young trapper or the pit in which he worked but his story could be repeated many times, not only in the Durham coalfield but in many other parts of industrial Britain during the first half of the nineteenth century. The story continued . . .

'He sits solitary by himself, and has no one to talk to him. He, however, sees every now and then the putters urging forward their trams through his gate, and derives some consolation from the glimmer of the little candle which is fixed on their trams. For he himself has no light. His hours, except at such times, are passed in total darkness. For the first week of his service in the pit his father had allowed him candles to light one after another, but the expense of 1p a-day was so extravagant expenditure out of 4p, the boy's daily wages, that his father of course withdrew the allowance the second week, all except one or two candles in the morning, and the week after the allowance was altogether taken away; and now, except a neighbour kinder than his father now and then drop him a candle as he passes, the boy has no light of his own.

'Thus hour after hour passes away, but what are hours to him, seated in darkness, in the bowels of the earth? He

knows nothing of the ascending or descending sun. Hunger, however, acts upon him, and he betakes to his bottle of coffee and slice of bread; and if desirous, he may have the luxury of softening it in a portion of the water in the pit, which is brought down for man and beast.

'His eyes are shut, and his ears fail to announce the approach of a tram. A deputy overman comes along, and a smart cut of his yard-wand at once punishes the culprit, and recalls him to his duty; and happy was it for him that he fell into the hands of the deputy overman, rather than one of the putters; for his fist would have inflicted a severer pain. The deputy overman moreover consoles him, by telling him that it was for his good that he punished him; and reminds him of boys well known to both, who when asleep had fallen down, and some had been severely wounded, and others killed. The little trapper believes that he is to blame, and makes no complaint; for he dreads being discharged; and he knows that his discharge would be attended with the loss of wages, and bring upon him the indignation of his father, more terrible to endure than the momentary vengeance of the deputy and the putters all taken together.

'Such is the day-work of the little trapper in the barrow-way. At last the joyful sound of "loose, loose" reaches his ears. The news of its being four o'clock, and of the order "loose, loose", having been shouted down the shaft, is by systematic arrangement sent for many miles in all directions round the farthest extremities of the pit. The trapper waits until the last

9

putter passes with his tram, and then he follows, and pursues his journey to the foot of the shaft, and takes an opportunity of getting into the cage and going up when he can. By five o'clock he may probably get home. Here he finds a warm dinner, baked potatoes, and broiled bacon lying above them. He eats heartily at the warm fire, and sits a little after. He dare not go out to play with other boys, for the more he plays the more he is sure to sleep the next day in the pit. He therefore remains quiet at home, until feeling drowsy, he then repeats the prayer taught by our blessed Lord, takes off his clothes, and is thoroughly washed in hot water by his mother, and is laid in his bed.

'The Saturday after pay-Friday is a holiday in the pit, and on that day the trapper lies in bed till between eight and nine. He rises and gets his breakfast, and then goes out to the highway to gather the manure of the horses to put on his father's potato garden. In the afternoon he indulges heartily in play, as he is not afraid of falling asleep next day, and of receiving the yard-wand of the deputy overman, or the fist of the putter.

'On Sunday he goes to the Sunday-school an hour before divine service. The fatigues of the week have left him but little spirit to attend to any learning, but his presence in school secures his presence in the place of worship. He returns and dines between twelve and one. He goes again to the Sunday-school, and attends divine worship. He gets tea *on his return. Then he walks out, and may be tempted to join other boys in some diversion. He returns home, says his prayers, undresses, washes, and gets into bed.'*

The South Durham coalfield lay between the rivers Wear and Tees and the area was described in the 1840s as being 'much intersected with railroads'. The same government inspector who described the young trapper's experience thought that the Durham countryside was not spoilt by the collieries. Indeed he expressed the opinion that the tall chimneys of the collieries as they gave off smoke and the steam from many engines were 'an ornament rather than an offence'.

Two of the largest pits in the coalfield were the Woodhouse Close Mine near Bishop Auckland and the Dorothea near Philadelphia. Dr. Mitchell the government inspector described the workings as being shaped like an old-fashioned window with many panes. The wooden sections representing the passages from which the coal was worked and the panes representing the pillars of coal left to support the roof. Such workings in the Durham coalfield lay from 120 feet to 700 feet below the surface.

Many of the collieries in the area were worked by the owners but the majority were let to companies who paid the owners royalties according to the amount of coal extracted. The colliery was managed in each instance by a person who usually had some knowledge of engineering. He was known as a coal-viewer. Beneath him was an under-viewer. Unlike some

11

other industrial areas where teams of men and boys extracted the coal, in the Durham coalfield each workman was individually paid. This system had given rise to further supervisors known as overmen, worth £100 a year, and to deputy overmen.

Coal-viewers admitted that they employed children from the age of nine years but evidence gathered proved that many children commenced work at five or six years of age. Sometimes it was the parents who requested that the children be employed so that the family income might be increased.

The following table gives details of the total number of trappers between the ages of 6 and 15 who worked in fifteen collieries in 1840:

COLLIERIES	AGES	NO. OF TRAPPERS
Hetton, North Hetton,	6 — 7	4
South Hetton,	7 — 8	12
East and West Rainton,	8 — 9	50
Pittington,	9 — 10	69
Broomside, Coundon,	10 — 11	53
Tees, Thornley, Sherburn,	11 — 12	25
Great Lumley, Newbottle	12 — 13	16
Cocken, Painshaw,	13 — 14	4
St. Helen's	14 — 15	2
Auckland		

One of these trappers was young Thomas Thew ten years of age. When asked, he did not know what month it was but said *'I have been a trapper six months. I likes it very much. I goes at five and come away at two, sometimes at three, as soon as the putters are done. The drivers have to feed the galloways after that. I get 20p a week and am quite content. Sometimes I falls asleep. If I'm caught at sleeping I gets a hiding with the yard-wand'*. The yard-wand was the stick by which an overman measured the distance from the coalface, where the putter loaded his tram, to the waggons drawn by horses in the main tunnel leading to the bottom of the shaft. The barrow way, as it was often known, where the putter worked was only about three to four feet high and had in the centre a narrow railway. On to this railway the putter placed his tram which consisted of a low platform on four wheels. The containers for coal were placed on the tram and filled by the putter, sometimes helped by the hewer — the miner who had cut the coal. The distance from the coalface to the rolley-way varied from a couple of hundred yards to as much as a mile and the putters were paid according to the number of journeys made, the cost increasing with the distance — hence the need of accurate measuring with the yard-wand.

William Laws was also ten years of age and worked in the Blackboy pit. *'I have been working two years. When I first went down I was a trapper in the barrow-way. I had a place to sit in and a candle and a string to pull the door. I liked it nicely. I get up at two o'clock when a man comes to call me and have coffee and cake before walking to the pit. I stop in the pit until four. I am now a trapper in the horseway where the doors are bigger. I have been baisted when a driver has told me to keep the door open as another horse was coming, and I have not done so. I like the pit nicely and get 4p a day. Sometimes I set mice-traps in the pit and catches two and bring them to the cat in the stable. There are midges in the pit that fly at the candles. The day I work in the pit I never play but other days I play marbles, or throw a ball against a wall. I play at touching a boy and running and trying to catch him. Sometimes I play with a wooden or iron hoop.'* William also described how there were so many trappers that the pit could not employ them all so the youngsters took it in turn to work. He himself usually worked about eight days in two weeks.

Between 1830 and 1840 many collieries were opened in South Durham and around each new colliery grew a village. Usually the houses were built by the colliery owner. Very often such houses were occupied before they had dried out and a high rate of mortality was thought to have resulted from the diseases contracted by moving in too soon. The village of Coxhoe which was close to the Clarence Hetton colliery was typical of many villages. The larger of two types of houses in this village cost £52 to build and consisted of a front room 14 feet by 14 feet 10 inches, a backroom 14 feet by 10 feet and, joining these two rooms, a pantry 6 feet 6 inches by 3 feet. The floor throughout was made of clay, lime and sand. Upstairs was a bedroom where the walls were only 2 feet 8 inches from the floor to a sloping roof. The distance from the top of the wall to the highest point of the roof was 7 feet. The height of the outside front wall was about 13 feet 10 inches. The other type of cottage consisted of one room and a pantry downstairs and one bedroom upstairs. These cost £42 each to build. Rental per annum on such cottages was about £5. Coxhoe in the 1840s had a population of some 5,000. It also had 30 beer shops, but no church or chapel, although both Wesleyan and Primitive Methodists arranged meetings in their own houses.

Here is an account of the expenditure of a miner's family, consisting of the man, his wife and two children for one week. The miner earned £1 a week.

	£ p.
One pound of blasting powder	5
One pound of candles for use in pit	4½
Soap	3
One pound and half sugar at 4p per lb.	6
Two ounces tea	2½
Quarter pound of coffee	3
One and a half stone (21 lbs) bread	10
Yeast, salt, pepper	1½
Seven pounds beef at 3p per lb	21
Pint of milk a day at ½p per pint	3½
Three quarter pound butter	5
One pound cheese	3
One pound bacon	3
Tobacco	3
	.74

He received his house free of rent but he had to pay 1p each week for coal. Board and lodging could usually be obtained for 45p, but single men usually paid 55p, and this included having the washing done and 'mending and darning' of clothes.

Today we regard the conditions under which people were employed during the last century as callous and unnecessary, yet many in those days were content to accept it as their lot. The inspector reported that in the Durham coalfield *'that the air agrees with human beings is proved by this fact, that when they go into the pits they require much more food to pacify their hunger. Persons previously lean when they go into pits become fat'.*

Northumberland and North Durham Collieries

From March to May 1841 the government inspector, one John Roby Leifchild, toured the Northumberland and north Durham collieries to obtain evidence. He wrote a very lengthy report the following September, but started by complaining of the difficulty in obtaining information. He declared that he could not talk to the youngsters underground because they were continually moving. He also blamed their use of mining phrases, their 'peculiar' accents and their being either stupid, or pretending to be, as further reasons for making his task difficult. He said that instead of answering his questions many of them put questions to him. Parents, too, either sent their children away on his approach or hid them.

Terms like 'putters', 'foals' and 'half-marrow' must have sounded like a foreign language to the gentleman from London. Putters were those who handled the trams of coal but these, in turn, could be foals who always went in front of the tram, or half-marrows who sometimes pulled or pushed, or headsmen who also pulled. These phrases were common to the north of England. In other parts of the country similar phrases became woven into the local dialects.

James Dagleish was one of three brothers working in the Howden Pit. He was almost thirteen years old and his brothers twelve and ten years. *'I am thirteen next Sunday. I have been down this pit three years. At first I kept a door then I went to putting but now I am a foal. I leave home at three and take ten minutes to walk to the pit. I come up about four. A month ago I stopped in the pit a double shift because other lads stopped. My back is sore with putting and my legs weak. Two and a quarter years ago the foul air fired a little and I got burnt on the face and hands. I was off six weeks. I cannot use my arms so well. They have lost their power; they are weak.'*

Robert Dixon, who also worked in the same mine, was nine years old. He had previously worked at Burdon Main colliery where he had kept a door but now he was a driver. *'The water in this pit is up to my knees in some places and the horses splash me. This is the only pit that works a night shift and I feel sleepy when I am on it. I have two brothers who are eleven and fourteen. One is a foal and the other a half-marrow. I cannot read or write'.*

One youngster did not know how old he was. This was Michael Wigham whose age was estimated to be about eight years. *'I keep a door in the Percy Pit. I get up at three o'clock and go down the pit about four. I ride down in a corf — six of us at a time. Some time ago when there was a double shift I worked on the night shift. I eat my bait about ten or midday. I go to Sunday school and chapel'.*

Many pits used corves. Frequently the men would sit in them with young children on their knees or the young children would cling to the rope. Sometimes a pit would use a chain the end of which was hooked back to form a loop in which two would stand.

Descending a pit was a natural occurrence for the workers but for others it was a novel experience which could be a talking point over dinner for a long time. The Gosforth colliery near Newcastle was sunk in 1825 but coal was not obtained until 1829 and then only after great expense. Some weeks later celebrations were held underground.

'The ballroom which was situated at the depth of nearly 1,100 feet below the surface of the earth, was in the shape of an L, the width of which was 15 feet, base 22 feet, and perpendicular 48 feet. Seats were placed on the side of the room, the floor was flagged, and the whole place was

brilliantly illuminated with lamps and candles. The company began to assemble and descend about half-past nine in the morning, and continued to do so until one in the afternoon. Immediately on their arrival at the bottom of the shaft, they proceeded to the face, that is the extremity of the drift, where each person hewed a piece of coal as a remembrance of the descent, and returned to enjoy the pleasures of the ballroom. As soon as a sufficient number of guests had descended, dancing commenced, and was continued without intermission till three o'clock in the afternoon, when all ascended once more to the upper regions in safety, much pleased and gratified with the amusements in which they had partaken. The Coxlodge band was in attendance; and cold punch, malt liquor, and biscuits of all kinds were in abundance. There were present between 200 and 300 persons, nearly one-half of whom were females'.

We have no record of what the workers at Gosforth colliery thought of such celebrations. Many of them no doubt accepted such eccentric behaviour as being perfectly normal for the owners and their friends. Many, however, must have looked with envy at the food and drink which was 'in abundance' and made comparisons with their own meagre rations.

George Anderson also worked in the Percy Pit where he was a door keeper. He was nearly eleven years of age. He and his sister were orphans and he gave his wages of 4p a day to his sister. *'I have worked in the night shift, every other fort-*

night, almost all the year. In the night shift I go down at 4 p.m. and come up about 4.30 in the morning. I'm often sleepy. I got my hammers twice by being asleep. The putters beat me with their soam-sticks (handles) and hurt me and made me cry because I did not open the doors for them. My door is nearly 2½ miles in. The pit looses at half past three and though I run a vast I am nigh an hour getting out. Once when I was driving a bad galloway and could not make it go on, George Hall, one of the foals, put some clots or lumps of stuff in my eyes and blinded me for a time and I had to lay idle all that day or work half work'.

The government inspector was very surprised that so many very young children were employed in the pits, and although some of the agents of the collieries claimed that they thought nine years of age was young enough for boys to commence work, the colliery returns showed that many younger children were employed.

There had been an explosion at the South Shields colliery in 1839 and 52 were killed. The father of James Forsyth was one of those who lost his life. James worked in the same pit and was one of the youngest, being only six years of age. The inspector thought he was not fit enough for work. James said *'I am a trapper. I go in very far bye. This is a very hot pit in bye. I was down at the explosion a year and a half ago; it came like a heavy wind and blew all the candles out, and the small coal about. It blew Richard Cooper down, and the door upon him'.*

Richard Cooper said *'I was cut in the head but not very bad. I would have been lost but one of the putters carried me out bye. It was just like somebody getting hold of my breeches and pulling them down. I am often bad. I have had fever and smallpox'*. Richard was indeed lucky not to have lost his life. Serious explosions could strip a man of all his clothing and the fact that Richard had had his trousers ripped from him was further proof of how terrible it must have been.

We have read how young boys were treated in north east England. In one way, perhaps, the girls were lucky as they were not taken underground to work except for instances in South Wales.

In some areas schools were provided for children and adults. This provision depended entirely on the coalowners. Some more enlightened owners even provided apprenticeships for keen and able employees. One of the first to do so was Sir John Guest of the Dowlais iron and coal complex at Merthyr Tydfil in South Wales.

Killingworth Schooling pit was one of a group owned by Lord Ravensworth. He had set up the Killingworth colliery schools for children of his employees. Here is one of the rules: *'The whole family of a subscriber be taught for 2½p per fortnight, excepting young men above 16 years of age, who shall subscribe 2½p for themselves; and the evening schools to find their own candles, which shall commence at 6 in the evening and continue until 8 o'clock'*. Not all the workmen subscribed to the school for it was not compulsory to do so.

In the infant department of the school, presided over by Mrs. Smith Goodger, there were 100 children. Here is a report of their day's activities: *'The average number of infants attending my school amount to 100, that is, male and female. The school opens in the morning with prayer at 9 o'clock, the children kneeling with folded hands, and eyes shut; at 10 o'clock all or part of a hymn or moral song sung; half an hour after 10 the Scriptures read by the mistress, and the children questioned on them; 11 o'clock exercise in the play-ground; next half hour the children formed into reading classes; 5 minutes to 12 grace before meat said or sung by the children. Afternoon the school opens with grace after meat, followed by the pence and multiplication-tables in rhyme; 3 o'clock exercise in the play-ground; half after 3 Commandments with responses; 5 minutes to 4 evening prayer. Various other exercises, too tedious to mention here, are used according to the discretion of teachers.'*

She also reported that *'when I first came, oaths were exceedingly common in the mouths of girls of 5 and 7 years of age; so much so that a special punishment for oaths was daily necessary. I fear they were infected by the language of the pit boys at their homes and they did not scruple at times to call me by the most opprobrious names that could be imagined. In the infant school they enter at 3 and leave at 5 years of age for the school of elder boys and girls. I think the bad language might be checked and suppressed by the parents who, instead of doing this, frequently abuse me for punishing the children'.*

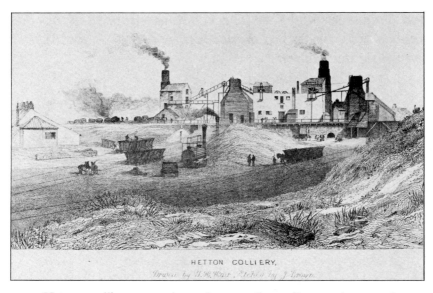

HETTON COLLIERY.
Drawn by T. H. Hair. Etched by J. Brown.

Hetton colliery was situated some five miles north-east of Durham. This view shows a typical colliery lay-out in the 1830s as drawn by Thomas Hair, long recognised for his accuracy when recording scenes. Wagons filled with coal are being drawn by horse from the pit and a railway engine stands nearby having been removed from the track probably to allow the shunting of horse drawn wagons to proceed. Workers' cottages are situated on the left. The headgear of the colliery can be seen in the background and the smoke rises from the furnaces of the boiler houses. The stone building on the left houses the boilers which operate the pumping engine. On the right is the building which houses the boilers which operate the winding engine

24

A contemporary view of the underground of a colliery near the pit bottom showing a hand operated crane which has lifted a corf from the wagon behind the horse and placed it on a tram which will be pushed into the cage before being raised to the surface. This is the type of passage known as a rolley-way in the north of England while the wheeled vehicle was known as a rolley.

COXLODGE, THE JUBILEE PIT.

Published by W. Fordyce Newcastle

Coxlodge colliery near Newcastle, named after the jubilee of George III. Typical colliers' cottages can be seen on the right. On the left coal is being loaded into a cart down a chute, probably for local sale. In the centre is a much larger chute down which comes the coal. It is then loaded into the railway wagons seen on the right

GARESFIELD COLLIERY.

Garesfield colliery was situated about seven miles south west from Newcastle and had been in production since 1800. The shaft was 150 feet deep. Today we associate coalmining with scenes of heavy industrialisation, In the early nineteenth century mines were often found in very rural settings as in the case of Garesfield. The two winding wheels of this pit can be clearly seen. The wagons on the right were hauled to the Tyne by horses and the coal transferred to ships by staiths.

PERCY PIT, PERCY MAIN COLLIERY.

The Percy pit was sunk in 1799 and was situated near North
Shields. This was the pit where Michael Wigham and George
Anderson worked (see text). The tall building in the centre
covers the shaft and the winding wheels can be clearly seen.
Tubs of coal are being moved in the centre of the illustration
and heat and light are being provided by a number of
braziers.

South Staffordshire

In some of the mining areas of Britain the owners employed contractors to get out the coal. These contractors were sometimes called 'charter-masters' but in south Staffordshire they were known as 'butties'. (The word spread to other parts of Britain, sometimes changing its meaning; for example, by this century a butty in the South Wales coalfield had become a trusted workmate or friend). In Staffordshire butties were men who had worked their way up from the lowliest tasks in a pit and managed to save enough money to buy from his capital tools to supply to the men and to purchase waggons and horses by which the pit could be worked.

A typical mine was outside Dudley on the Stourbridge road at a place called Holly Hall. A small wooden platform called a 'skip', held by a chain at each corner, was the method by which the miners were lowered into the pit. Light was provided by candles stuck in clay. At the bottom of the shaft the tunnel was about eight feet wide and nine feet high with a tramroad running down the centre for the horse-drawn waggons. At the end of the main tunnel was a smaller passageway and in here miners worked lying on their sides and undercutting the coal to a height of about two feet, leaving small pillars of coal to support the rest. Young boys were clearing away the coal from the undercutting process. Finally the pillars were cut away and the whole came crashing down under its own weight. Very often the miners failed to move away quickly enough and this could result in death or at least serious injury.

In Staffordshire the mines worked one shift from six in the morning until six at night with an hour's break for lunch. The wives often brought the men's food to the pit about midday and it was sent down on the skips. The inspector described how for lunch *'the miners congregate in a large dining room cut out of the coal, naked from the waist up, eating, drinking and laughing'*. It is difficult to imagine young children wanting to do anything but sleep at this time. Sometimes each man would be given a quart of ale called pit beer, and the boys a pint.

Employed in this coalfield were 'air door boys' whose job it was to open and close the doors which controlled the mine ventilation. Those who moved the carriages from the coalface to the horse ways were called 'pushers'. Little boys in particular were used to rake up the small coal left after the large pieces had been loaded. This small coal was called 'slack' and was sometimes used to fill in the spaces where the coal had been removed. This area was called the 'gob' and so the work of the boys as they threw the slack into the space, was called 'gobbing'.

Girls were not employed down in the pit but they were often to be found at the top of the shaft where they unloaded the coal from the skips. They were known an 'bankwomen' after the name given to the surface of the pit which was called the 'bank'.

John Greaves had started work at seven years of age opening doors. When the inspector spoke to him he said *'I carry dirt back from the men into the gob. Every boy has to clear away for two men and if he do not do it they strap him. I dare not say much about it, for fear of them giving me more and perhaps master turning me off* (dismissing him) *A boy who keeps two men clear gets 10p a day. It is the butties' apprentices who are worst used. These lads are made to go where other men will not let their children go. If they will not do it they take them to the magistrates who commit them to prison. One butty has a beer shop and if you do not go to his shop to drink he will stop your employment'.* A young man by the name of Joseph Dyke, a friend of John Greaves, told the inspector that all this was true. Greaves went on to say that *'the head master* (the butty) *keeps a tommy-shop* (food store) *and the butty will tell us plainly that if we do not tommy enough we shall not have more work.'*

In south Staffordshire there were also iron mines where children worked. One of these was Thomas Rogers who had started work at nine years of age. *'I drew with a girdle and chain. I suffered great misery. My skin was chafed very much so I wrapped my shirt around the sore place. I had my skin hurt for weeks together. It was very cruel work. It is entirely done with now in this part of the country.'*

The girdle and chain was used in many parts of Britain for hauling loads and children hated it for the reason given by Thomas Rogers. It usually consisted of a rope, chain and small hook. The rope was worn around the waist and passed between the legs to the chain and hook. Many of the colliery managers told the government inspectors that they did not allow its use in their pits, but when the children were interviewed it appeared the managers were not always truthful.

Mention has already been made of the skips used for raising and lowering coal, men and boys. The system was very dangerous and many lost their lives by falling down the shaft. The skips were often raised by a horse gin (as shown in diagram) in the small mines. The gin driver was usually a young lad, or even a young girl. Alongside the track, made by the horse as it went around, was a small shelter made of bits and pieces and alongside that a fire. During cold weather the boy or girl would stand near the fire and control the horse by throwing stones at it.

South Gloucestershire and North Somerset Coalfields

A different inspector visited each of these coalfields but as their findings were very similar we shall deal with both areas together.

Unlike pits in Scotland and South Wales no girls or women were employed in these coalfields. Young boys were used for many of the colliery activities. There were those who opened and shut the doors — the trappers we have already heard about — then there were 'pushers' who pushed or pulled the coal trams, and others who helped to turn the 'guy' wheel, the wheel which operated at the top of an underground slope or incline. It helped to heave loaded coal carts up a slope from the coalface towards the bottom of the shaft. In appearance it looked like a windlass.

Coal had been mined in south Gloucestershire for many generations before 1840, particularly in the Kingswood and Coal pit Heath areas. The coal seams varied from one foot to about six feet in thickness. Where coal was being mined in a one foot thick seam young boys were used, for the space was too narrow for an adult. One of the most hated pieces of equipment in the pits in this area was the chain and girdle.

The Golden Vale colliery was one of those owned by the Holelane coal company. One of the boys working there was William Short who was eleven years of age. *'The girdle used to hurt me but not now. I earn 1½p a day carting. I never heard the other boys complain'*. The inspector examined William and found that he had bruises on his loins. Some of the boys would place rags between their bodies and the chain to prevent chafing. One manager compared the boys to young horses who are bruised when they first wear harness such as a collar. He thought it 'quite natural' that they should wear the girdle for drawing the coal.

John Beard who was nine years of age worked at the Middle pit which was one of those owned by the Radstock Coal Company. *'I began work three-quarters of a year ago. I haul with my uncle and another man called Sedge Chappell who is sixty. I start work in the morning at four and comes up generally from two to four. I carry bread and cheese and stops to eat two or three times. None of the men or boys have punished me badly'.*

Thomas Milson worked for the same company at the Ludlass pit and was ten years of age. *'I goes down generally at four and often bides till four or five. I'm one of the last to come up. I take something to eat and catch time to eat it two or three times'.*

Samuel Latchum was also ten and worked in the same pit as Thomas Milson. He said that he had never been beaten, but that he had seen other boys of his own size beaten by the carters. There is no doubt that a great deal of bullying took place in the pits, adding to the misery of some of those who worked there.

Swearing was commonplace and in some of the mines there was a system of fines when a person was caught. The usual fine was 2½p, a great deal of money in those days. Very often the money went into a sick fund to help those unable to work.

The inspector for south Gloucestershire described how he usually tried to interview workers as they reached the surface at the end of a shift. He described how one little 'urchin' emerged with his father. The boy was only seven and a half and according to the father had been working at the pit, the

34

coal works at Lower Easton, for twelve months. The inspector thought the lad *'looked grotesque and revolting . . . a pigmy collier'*.

It was in this pit that the manager had made a metal container of iron plates bolted together in which the miners stood to be lowered or raised. This was the fore-runner of a modern cage. The most common rope was made of hemp and the most popular was a flat rope so called because three or four smaller ropes were laid side by side. Wire ropes could not be twisted for the impurities in the metal caused them to snap. Different areas preferred different methods and we shall see how, in Devon and Cornwall, a system of ladders was used for descending into the mines.

East Scotland Coalfield

We have seen something of the terrible conditions under which young children had to work and live. In many ways they were well-off compared to the boys and girls, men and women who worked in the mines in Scotland. Until 1775 most of those who worked for land owners were virtually slaves and could be punished severely by their masters; they could not change their employer. An act of Parliament in 1775 was intended to do away with this system but in many cases it failed to do so. Landowners who started mining on their lands simply applied the agricultural system of bondage to the mines and so *'Colliers and coalbearers are in a state of slavery and bondage'*. Eventually all colliers were declared free men but it took many years for the old system to disappear. At the time of our story there was far more suffering among the people of Scotland who worked in the mines than probably anywhere else in Britain.

Although we have been reading about young children, we must remember that if they did not become involved in an accident, then they might spend the whole of their lives in the pits. One such person was a forty year-old coal-bearer Jane Peacock Watson who worked in West Linton, Peebleshire. *'I have wrought in the bowels of the earth 33 years. I have been married 23 years and had nine children, six are alive and three died of typhus a few years since. Have had two dead born. Horse-work ruins the women; it crushes their haunches, bends their ankles and makes them old women at 40. Women so soon get weak that they are forced to take the little ones down to relieve them; even children of six years of age do much to relieve the burthen'.* At the same pit was a six year-old who also carried coal. The inspector described her as a most *'interesting and perfectly beautiful child'.* On being interviewed she said *'I have been down six weeks and make 10 to 14 rakes a day; I carry a full 56 lbs. of coal in a wooden backit. The work is na guid; it is so very fair. I work with sister Jesse and mother; dinna ken the time we gang; it is gai dark. I get plenty of broth and porridge, and run home and get bannock, as we live just by the pit'.*

Another little girl, this time 11 years of age, was Betsy Sharp who worked in the Elphingston Colliery in the parish of Tranent. She worked with her mother, brother and four sisters. *'I first wrought on the Edge Seams at Drum near Gilmerton but I've been carrying coal and putting here for three years. Father is dead; it was the bad breath that killed him. I dinna ken how old he was; he was na very old'.* 'Bad breath' explained many illnesses that resulted in death more often than not. These illnesses ranged from bronchitis to tuberculosis.

Mines could be cold and dry, cold and wet, hot and wet or hot and dry depending on many conditions. The New Craighall colliery in the parish of Inveresk was wet, as was reported by a horse driver of 11 years, Robert Thompson. *'I have done eighteen months and I work 12 or 14 hours* (a day). *I would like it fine if the time would allow me to see the daylight. The pit is very wet and sair drappie. The women complain of the wet, but they are obliged to like it'.* If a pit was very wet then pumps might be installed as at this one. The pump boy was only 10 years of age, named Alexander Gray. *'I pump out the water in the under bottom of the pit, to keep the men's rooms dry. I am obliged to pump fast or the water would cover me. I had to run away a few weeks go, as the water came up so fast that I could no pump at all, and the men were obliged to gang. The water frequently covers my legs and those of the men when they sit to pick. I bring pieces of oaten bread with me. I know the hours. The minute hand is larger than the one that points to the hour. I know I work 12 and 14 hours, as I can tell by the clock. I go down at three, sometimes five in the morning and come up at six or seven in the night'.*

Although Alexander's work was hard, it is doubtful if he would have changed places with Catherine Thompson, aged 11, who worked in the Redding collieries in Stirlingshire. She was rather deaf, caused, so she said, by a caning *'across the head'* she received in school when she was six. *'I work with my sister who is 13. We start at six in the morning and return at six at night. We both work on father's account and draw his coal. The hutchies* (carts) *hold 8 cwt. which we have first to fill before we draw. The distance we draw is said to be a full 1,000 yards. I suffer much from pains in my knee, which was crushed some time ago by a hutchie'.* Opening one of the doors for Catherine was 7 year-old David Gay. *'I gang at half four in the morning and come up at half six at night. I can hardly get up the stairs-pit when work is done'.* Poor David, although he found difficulty in climbing the ladders to the surface, some children a little older than he had to climb the same ladders with loads of coal on their shoulders. Also in Stirlingshire in the Somerhouse collieries was Agnes Marshall, a 10 year-old putter, who was helped by her sister of eight and her brother not quite seven. *'We draw with ropes and chains. We do not like the pit nor the work, it is aching, but father says we shall like it when we are used to it'.*

In the Banknock colliery in Stirlingshire was Hugh Campbell whose evidence showed that cruelty existed there also. *'I have helped to fill father's hutchies 12 months; sometimes I shove them with my brother. If I do not do my bidding I get my licks, sometimes the belt and whiles the pick-shaft'.*

Some of the pits employed very few people, such as Castle Bigg colliery in the county of Perth where 18 worked; five of these were females. The pit was 78 feet deep and access was gained by a stair pit. All the coal brought to the surface was carried on the backs of three of the five women who spent the whole of their working day ascending and descending the stair pit. The coal would be carried in a basket on the shoulders, the basket being supported by a rope which passed around the carrier's head on the forehead. The clothing of these and other women was usually made of a coarse hemp or sacking and rarely was this garment washed, instead it was hung up to dry on arriving home in preparation for the next day's work. A cap of the same material was usually worn on the head. Stockings only covered the ankles and calves, and shoes were a luxury for some of those who hauled the hutchies or slypes.

On arriving home many of the workers found conditions just as bad. Unlike the houses in Durham, which were apparently neat and clean, in Scotland there was a *'deplorable picture of filth and poverty'*. The house, if indeed it could be called that, consisted of one room about 10 or 12 feet square, which might hold six to ten people. There would be one or two bed-steads with no covering, a few stools and some chipped crockery. Fowls, pigs, dogs or a donkey might also share the room.

The inspector was told that the lack of furniture was a help rather than a hindrance if the miner decided to *'flit'*, that is, to change his place of work suddenly. The homes possessed no water or drainage and all waste was placed outside the front door. The inspector *'believed it was usual for them* (the workers) *to wash their faces once in the day after labour, and sometimes the children followed the example'*.

The food of these families consisted largely of oaten cake, oaten bread or porridge. *'Butcher's meat'* was an unknown commodity and even those who cut the coal did not receive beer as in some parts of the country. Children usually drank the water available, often in too great quantities, in the mines. There is no doubt that the Scottish miners were far worse off than others in Britain due in no small measure to the serf-like system which had existed for so long.

Even in death the miners were almost ignored. In Bo'ness colliery in Linlithgowshire worked Mary Sneddon, aged 15 and a putter. Her brother worked in the pit with her and had been killed a few months before the government inspector visited. She said *'a piece of roof fell on his head* (her brother) *and he died instantly. He was brought home, coffined and buried in Bo'ness Kirkyard. No one came to inquire about how he was killed. They never do in this place'*. Mary's story could be repeated many times.

Let us leave Scotland with the words of the overseer of Teases colliery in the parish of Largo in Fife, one William Graham: *'I think a limitation of the age which children should work in mines would be harmful, as they ought to*

begin young. Boys get injured through carelessness; one was
killed a short time since by bad air'.

There were many people like William Graham and
unfortunately those who suffered the most were the children
who worked for such people.

Figure 1   A circular ladder system frequently found in the east
                  Scotland coalfield.

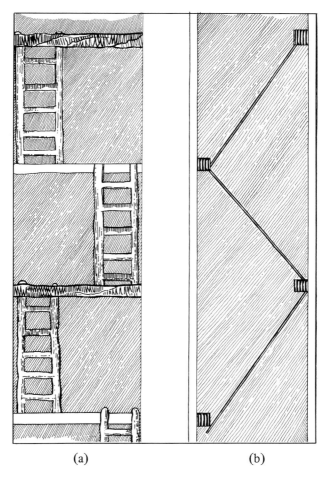

(a)	(b)

Figure 2   Two views of the same ladder system in a shaft.
a) front view
b) side view
Very often on each landing when a person would transfer from one ladder to another there would be a trapdoor in the floor

43

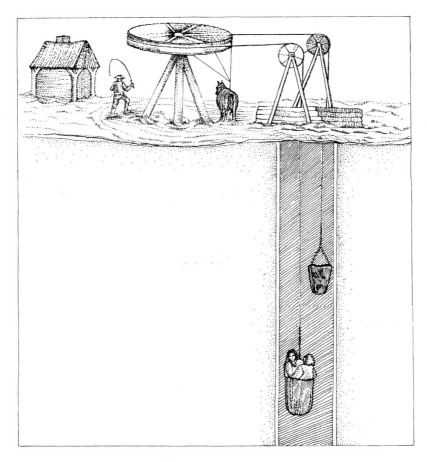

Figure 3   Human power was sometimes replaced by horse power as in the case of the horse gin shown here. By a system of wheels two baskets are being operated at once, one being raised and the other lowered. Sometimes only one wheel was used and this would raise or lower a small platform attached by each corner to the main rope

Figure 4   The pits of the Pembrokeshire coalfield in the early nineteenth century were not very deep and windlasses were used to lift coal and workers. Teams of women were employed to do the winding. The men refused to do such work.

A water balance pithead gear as it was in Rhymney, Gwent, in 1934. It now stands outside the National Museum of Wales in Cardiff. The balance gear was worked by placing water in a tank under the empty tram on the surface, while the tank under the full tram at the bottom of the pit was left empty. On releasing the brake, the full tram and the empty tank were raised to the surface and the empty tram and full tank of water were lowered to the bottom where the water would be run off, usually to a drainage adit, or otherwise pumped back to the surface. In the first half of the nineteenth century there were well over one hundred of these pits in Glamorgan and Monmouthshire using water balances. Underneath the left hand side of the wheel can be seen the rods by which the tank was supported. On the right hand side the winding chain can be seen disappearing into the pit shaft.

46

Raising coal underground by means of a windlass. The full
tubs were partly balanced by the empties. This was the
method usually adopted on underground slopes or inclines.

Mines in Devon and Cornwall

So far we have read how children worked in coal mines more than 130 years ago, but we must remember that other sorts of mines existed, sometimes close to the coal mines. For example, lead was taken from the ground in North Durham and iron ore pits were to be found in East Scotland. The mines of Devon and Cornwall were worked for such ores as copper, tin, manganese and lead, and although these ores were perhaps cleaner than coal, very similar conditions and dangers existed for the work people. Most of the mines in the area were referred to as being wet due to the presence of a great deal of water. This had to be pumped out by steam engines. If a mine was near the sea it was usual to run the water off to the sea.

In the West Country it was the custom to use ladders in the shaft for ascending and descending. The ladders were usually no more than thirty feet long with the rungs one foot apart. Wooden ladders were preferred to iron ones, for the ladder rusted very easily, especially in the copper mines. Whenever possible oak would be used — the wreck of a ship often provided a source of timber. The ladders were placed at an angle so that for very six foot length the distance from the wall increased by about two feet six inches. The angle formed allowed the workmen to climb almost standing up straight. Between each ladder was a platform called a sollar and in the platform was a man-hole to descend to the next ladder. Sometimes the man-hole would have a cover to prevent anything or anyone falling through.

One of the young boys who did not have to go down into the mine was nine year old Richard Jeffery who worked at the Consolidated Copper Mines at Gwennap. *'My father died of the cholera in Mexico and I live with my mother and three sisters two and a half miles away from here. I get 30p a month working at the 'boxes' '.* The boxes were tables where the copper ore was separated from the stone *'my hands get sore when I am long at the 'shambles' '.* This was the heap of stones left after the ore had been cleaned.

Cleaning the different types of ores was a boring but important task done by both boys and girls. The work was known as dressing and the person in charge as the Captain of the Dressers. At the Cornubian Lead Mine the captain reported *'The boys on the surface were very badly behaved when I came here a twelve month since. They were constantly pelting and splashing each other and hooting at passers-by. I told them I would discharge the first offender and it was soon put a stop to. They have become much more quiet of late and for the past three months they have held a meeting at dinner time among themselves at which they sing hymns and have prayers'.* For such a change to take place was remarkable, and one wonders if they had been terrified by the threat of losing their jobs. At 10 am. the children who worked on the surface were allowed a ten minute break known as 'crowst'. It was at this time that they might eat a 'hoggan', also known as 'hobban' or 'fuggan', a pastie containing potato and sometimes pieces of pork. One agent reported that he had *'seen some of the girls steal away to eat this meal behind a hedge, ashamed of the meanness of their fare'.*

Those who worked underground changed their dress before going down for woollen trousers, shirt and jacket. They wore thick leather shoes but no stockings. On their heads they wore thick felt broad-brimmed hats weighing about two pounds. A lump of clay holding a candle was then attached.

The ore was usually removed by blasting it out with gunpowder. An iron bar with a wedge shape at one end was driven into the 'face' where the ore was being removed. As the bar was being driven in with a mallet it would also be rotated by hand by one of the team of workmen. The next stage was to ram gunpowder down the hole and then a length of fuse was attached. The gunpowder was held in place by packing a particular type of clay into the hole. This also stopped the force of the explosion coming back down the hole but kept it 'inside' thus releasing more ore.

Teams of men contracted to remove the rock and this was called 'tutwork'. They were paid according to an agreed sum for a certain height removed. Another method was known as 'tribute'. This was the system whereby the men removed the rock and prepared the ore for market. They were then paid a percentage in the pound on the total for which the ore was sold. Those who lived on this system lost badly when the market was poor but when the market was good *received a sum unusually large for their rank in life'.*

The wetness of the mines, and the particles of minerals released by explosion, contributed to very bad conditions. Tuberculosis or consumption was rife among the workers. For example, of the 67 miners who died in the parish of St. Just in one year, 29 died of consumption, 16 by accident in the mines and only 9 from 'old age'. The average age of those who died by accident was 21 ¼ years.

Joseph Roberts was nearly fifteen and worked at the East Wheal Rose Lead Mine. Horses were never used in the mines of Devon and Cornwall so Joseph wheeled barrows full of ore to the bottom of the shaft where it would be raised to the surface by a 'kibble', an iron bucket. Joseph said *my work is rolling stuff and I get £1.25 a month. All the ground must be removed by shooting* (blasting). *There is a good deal of powder smoke and sometimes I cannot draw my breath. Sometimes I cough and I spit black stuff. I bring a pasty for my dinner but they do not send any water down this mine so I get thirsty'.* This was obviously a dry mine which in some ways was an advantage. We do not know what happened to Joseph but the 'coughing' he mentioned and the 'black stuff' might well have been a sign of serious illness.

Another lad who complained of the same trouble was 13 year old Absalom George, who worked at the Fowey Consuls Mine which produced copper. *'I work with my father and get my wages as 'part of a man'. When I come up I spit nasty black trade. Sometimes I carry up borers and other weights which makes me pant a good deal'.* Absalom's father had a small farm and the boy was one of seven children.

Very often the father and all the children would work, as in the case of a family from the parish of Gwennap. Mother and father were 45 years old and 47 years old respectively. Four of their children had died and one was married. Here is their income for one month:

	£	p.
Father (47)	2	55
Constance (21)		75
John (19)	2	00
Richard (17)	1	30
James (14)		80
Elizabeth (12)		10
	7	50

The numbers in brackets are their ages.
The same family's expenses for one month were:

	£	p.
Flour, barley, soap, starch, tea, butter	3	50
Coal and candles		40
Meat	1	00
Shoes and clothes	1	25
Sundries		75
	6	90

Many of the mining districts in the area had 'clubs'. To the club a miner would contribute 7½p a month and a woman would pay 1p for every 50p she earned. If a miner became ill the club would pay him £1.50 a month or a woman 60p a month. On the death of a miner his next of kin received £5. Such help as this was uncommon at the time in the industrial areas of Britain but was to become very popular towards the end of the century.

Compared to many other parts of Britain conditions for children in Devon and Cornwall were better, although by any standards they were terrible and should never have been tolerated.

Yorkshire Coalfield

One of the areas in Britain where conditions in the mines were at their worst was in Yorkshire.

John Hobson worked in the Sheffield Soap Pit: *'I was five when I first went into the pit. I trapped the door when I first went and then hooked the corves on the gin and I now hurry and help to fill* (the corves). *They don't use me ill except when I miss marking the number of the corve, then they give a bit of pick shaft'*.

In the same pit was John Saville, a seven year old trapper. *'I stand and open and shut the door. I'm generally in the dark and sit me down against the door. I stop twelve hours in the pit. I never see daylight except on Sundays. I fell asleep one day and a corve ran over my leg and made it smart. They'd squeeze me against the door if I fell to sleep again. When I go home I wash myself and get my drinking* (a local term for tea). *I've sometimes dry bread, sometimes bread and cheese, sometimes red herring and potato to my dinner in the pit'.*

Boys and girls worked in a variety of jobs. The 'hurriers' moved the coal from the face (where the coal was cut) to the horse-ways or to the bottom of the shaft. Frequently they might come to an incline so steep that a pulley system had been placed there. This would be operated by jinny-boys who had to wind up the full corves and steady the empty ones as they passed down the incline. The corves or trams ran on wheels of about 9 or 12 inches diameter. The corve was oblong in shape and varied in size, holding anything from 2 to 10 cwt. of coal.

Tramming was another name given to the pushing of the corves. An example of the distance to be 'hurried' was at Messrs. Hopwood and Jackson's colliery, Barnsley, where a corve held 7 cwt. of coal and had to be moved 400 yards. Each boy or girl was expected to make 20 trips in a shift. The chain and girdle was also used in some pits. The vicar of Boldestone, the Reverend William Irving, reported that in the nearby Webster's Pit there were 36 girls employed in hurrying. All wore trousers and could hardly be distinguished from the boys. Very often the hurriers were paid by the collier who cut the coal.

Maria Gooder worked in Thorpe's pit at Gawber. *'I hurry for a man with my sister Anne who is going 18. He is good to us. I don't like being in the pit. I am tired and afraid. I go at 4.30 after having porridge for breakfast. I start hurrying at 5. We have dinner at noon. We have dry bread and nothing else. There is water in the pit but we don't sup it. Sometimes the men let us have a little beer, but not always. I think we hurried two dozen corves today'.*

Colliers who wanted children to work for them sometimes went to the workhouse. This happened in Batley where, in 1840, a lad by the name of Thomas Townsend was taken to the Thornhill colliery. His date of birth was given as 1836 which made him four years of age when taken into the pit to work. He was, however, returned to workhouse later because of stealing. Another very young child at work was Ann Firth who had commenced at 6 years of age. She lived at Middlestown and worked at the Woodenthorpe Pit at Flockton. *'It's wet and I get my feet wet. Ann Eyre hurries with me and she is younger. I am tired in my arms and my legs, and all. I don't like being in pit'.*

A lad of 13 years of age, working in Tinker's Day-hole pit at Hepworth, went by the name of Ebenezer Healey. *'I went down into a pit to help before I was five. I used to thrust but now I hurry with belt and chain. There are no rails and I have to hurry full corves up hill as well as down. I do 16 runs a day and I get 5p. There are girls that hurry in the same way with belt and chain. Our breeches are often torn between the legs with the chain. I thrash my brother a little sometimes but it don't hurt him. I do nought but lug him a bit when he stops* (pulls his hair). *The girls get thrashed as well as the boys'*. The evidence given by Ebenezer does not paint a very pretty picture.

There were no regular holidays in the pits except perhaps at Christmas when they would close for a day or two. Sundays were intended for recreation but for most, particularly the children, it was an opportunity to stay in bed and rest in readiness for a new week.

The inspector who visited the Yorkshire Coalfield was a Mr. J.C. Symons and he was of the opinion that children were saying what they thought he would like to hear. For example most young children kept on repeating that they were 'never tired'. No doubt they suspected that they might otherwise be dismissed. The inspector was also of the opinion that far more ill-treatment of children went on than the workers and management were prepared to admit.

The coal owners were afraid too — afraid that Parliament would pass laws that would interfere with the cheap labour system, with its lack of safety and complete disregard for decent standards. Typical of the coal owners in Britain, the Yorkshire owners wrote a letter to the government after the inspector had paid a visit in which they claimed that to keep *'books and registers for weekly examination . . . would mean serious interruption and delay in carrying on of mines'* and *'to attempt to extend a compulsory system of education to children employed in mines would be fruitless'*. It was to be many years before conditions were to improve, not only for young children but for adults as well.

The words of one little lad William Firth, aged six and working in the Dial Wood Pit at Flockton, seem to convey a little of the misery of those who worked in the mines at the time. *'I hurry with my sister and they pay me sometimes. I don't like to be in pit. It tires me a great deal. I was crying to go out this morning'*.

A young girl hauling a tub of coal in the barrow-way by means of a rope and chain, sometimes referred to as a chain and girdle. It was in common use throughout coalfields in Britain, although when interviewed most colliery managers denied that they permitted its use. Unlike the illustration here the chain usually passed underneath the body between the legs.

The Crawshay family came from Yorkshire and owned iron-works and mines around Merthyr Tydfil in South Wales. Here is one of their typical three-roomed cottages at Rhydycar, on the outskirts of the present town, built about 1810 and still occupied. The roof at the back of this type of house continued to within about six feet of the ground, giving an extra bedroom and a larder.

Cottages for the workers were usually built by the Company owning a colliery and catered only for the basic need of protection from the weather. This photograph shows Upper Rank Row, Blaenavon, Gwent, built in the 1820s. The ground floor consisted of a kitchen and bedroom and the first floor of one large bedroom. Many of the occupiers of these houses kept animals such as poultry or pigs to supplement their diet hence the stable type doors. This row of houses was demolished about 1972.

The South Wales Coalfield

The South Wales coalfield extends in a wide band from Pontypool in Gwent to the coast of St. Bride's Bay in Dyfed. At the time of our story the coal mines were generally located on the rim of the coalfield, especially on the north side between Aberdare and Blaenavon. The coal was mined to feed the furnaces of the early iron works which were numerous in the area.

Many of the mines were entered by the traditional shaft with either ladders attached to the sides or a platform raised and lowered by a horse gin. Because of the mountainous nature of the land many of the mines were entered by a tunnel which ran into the side of the mountain. These were called 'levels'. Many children when they were frightened could leave the mine far more easily if they worked in this type. The Plymouth mines near Merthyr Tydfil consisted of many 'level' type pits where coal was worked to feed the great ironworks. Susan Reece was six years of age and was a door keeper in one of the pits. *'I have been below six or eight months and I don't like it much. I come here at six in the morning and leave at six at night. When my lamp goes out or I am hungry I go home. I haven't been hurt yet'.*

In one colliery in Gwent, namely the Gwrhay, which was entered by means of a level, evidence was given by many young children. Moses Williams was a seven year old air-door boy. *'Father carried me down eighteen months since. I keep an air-door. He brings me in the morning and I return*

60

with him at night'. Rosser Jenkins was a year older. *'I work with my father as often as he does. We sometimes work a long time. He sometimes takes bread and cheese and we drink the water below'.* This pit was a wet one which added to the boy's misery. In the same pit was a seven year old lad employed as a collier, that is, he actually cut the coal. His name was Richard Hutton. *'I have worked here for a year. The place is 'middling' (reasonable). I'm glad when I get home. The shooting used to frighten me and I still don't like it'.* The shooting Richard refers to were the explosions as the coal was blasted from the coal face.

John Evans was an eight year old collier also in the same mine: *'I've been down two years. Father took me down to claim a dram. I often fall asleep and father pulls me up when he wants me'.* The miners were paid by results so even John Evans's help could count towards an extra dram resulting in a small increase in wages.

The part owner of this pit was a person by the name of Aaron Crossfield. He told the inspector that he thought the youngest child employed there was eight years of age. He also stated that both day and night schools were operated by him but the inspector failed to obtain evidence to support this. There is little doubt that untruths were told by management in many of the pits.

Another mine in Gwent was the 180 foot deep Buttery Hatch. An eight year old collier here was William Skidmore.

He himself did not know his age but his father thought it was eight years. *'I don't know when I first went down, it is so long since. The place where I work is very wet. I got my hand crushed a short time since by a piece of roof falling and it kept me idle for a short time. I have seven brothers and sisters. I go to Sunday School where I have learned my a, b, c'.*

The steward of the colliery, a Mr. John Jeremiah, was certain that William had been 'down four years'. This meant he had started work at four years of age. The steward also said that a seven years old collier had been down at least three years. The reasons given for this terrible state of affairs were the low wages and the high cost of food. These reasons were put forward by a minister in the district, a Reverend Edward Jenkins, who ran a small school which was supported by the coppers of the miners. The minister himself had two boys working in the mine, one of seven and the other fourteen years of age. The average wage of adult colliers in the mine was 70p a week out of which they had to pay the cost of powder and candles. There were numerous cases where both mine and shop were owned by the same person. In some places rarely was money paid as wages but the shop record book and the mine book would be checked on pay day and if a balance was in favour of the collier then he was paid in goods. The system was open to abuse. It was not unknown for miners to go to the shop, obtain goods and pay for drink at a public house with the goods. In some schools the fees were paid in provisions obtained from the mine owner's store.

The chain and girdle already referred to in other coalfields was used in South Wales also. Those who used it to draw the carts of coal were called carters and they worked in the low passageways between the coalface and the higher and wider tunnels where horses might be used. Those children who took food into the mine ate it as they worked, for wages depended on results and time spent eating was regarded in terms of loss of wages. The carts held about 1½ cwt. of coal and would be dragged a distance of anything between 20 and 50 yards in a height rarely exceeding 3 feet. For this a carter would earn no more than 5p a day.

Housing conditions were as bad in South Wales as anywhere in the country. The iron works and coal mines at Merthyr Tydfil had attracted thousands of workers and their families. Many ended up working in the pits and it was not unknown for three or four families to occupy a two or three roomed house. Consequently there could be a dozen or more sleeping in one room. One toilet had to suffice for a number of cottages, assuming that there was one. This lack of even the most elementary sanitation facilities was responsible for cholera epidemics occurring from time to time during hot summers. Three took place in 1849, 1854 and 1866. The last commenced with the first case reported on 22 August, the patient dying two days later. The eleventh case, a Mrs. Connolly, the wife of an Irish labourer, was taken ill on the 28 August and died on the 1 September. This is how the official report described the case:

'The family Connolly occupied the house No.9 Sunny Bank, it is a small four-roomed house — total cubic space of the three sleeping rooms about 1200 feet. Here thirteen persons slept nightly. The wife was first seized; to her bedroom was a small window about 18 inches square, outside was a heap of ashes saturated with putrifying house slops. Eight others of this family were attacked within five days; they were removed to the Cholera Hospital'.

The report goes on to say that Mrs. Connolly probably caught the disease by visiting No.16 Sunny Bank occupied by a tailor whose wife also died. The habits of those in No.16 were described in the report as being *'intemperate and dirty'* while the *'cesspool in the garden was overflowing and the floor of the sleeping room thickly covered with dirt and filth'.* (See Pages 66 and 67. Table XVII taken from report by Thomas Dyke, Medical Officer of Health, Merthyr Tydfil).

Working women and girls were often too tired to perform the normal domestic duties of caring for a home.

The Dowlais iron works at this time were the largest in the world and supplied products to dozens of countries. The company also owned iron and coal mines. In one of the coal mines there were three young girls. Elizabeth Williams, aged ten who had been at work one year and sisters Mary and Rachel Enoch, eleven and twelve years respectively. *'We are door-keepers in the four foot level. We leave the house before six each morning and are in the level until seven*

Cholera at Merthyr-Tydfil.
RETURN OF CASES,
TUESDAY, JULY 31, 1849.

	ATTACKED.	DEAD.
MERTHYR.		
Total from commencement (May 25th), as per last Report, corrected by Registration Returns up to 10 A. M., Yesterday	1415	593
New Cases, up to 10 A. M., To-day	18	12
DOWLAIS.		
Total from commencement (June 10th), up to 10 A. M., Yesterday	536	231
New Cases, up to 10 A. M., To-day	23	8
ABERDARE.		
Total from commencement (June 24th), up to 10 A. M., Yesterday	211	36
New Cases, up to 10 A. M., To-day	8	4
TOTAL	2211	884

FRANK JAMES,

TABLE XVII. *Abstract of First Cases of*

No.	When taken ill.	When died.	Where died.	Sex	Age	Occupation
1	22nd August	24th August	15, David square, Abercannaid	M.	36	Wife of Puddler (Welsh)
2	22nd ,,	25th ,,	57, Quarry row, Tydfil's Well	F.	45	Wife of Fireman (Irish)
3	23rd ,,	25th ,,	31, do do	M.	32	Fireman (Welsh)
4	23rd ,,	26th ,,	13, Morris court, Merthyr	F.	75	Rag cleaner (Irish)
5	24th ,,	25th ,,	7, Cwm Canol street, Dowlais	M.	21	Hooker in Iron Mills (Irish)
6	24th ,,	25th ,,	1, Flag & Castle ct., Dowlais	M.	8	Son of Labourer (English)
7	24th ,,	1st September	16, Sunny Bank, Tydfil's Well	F.	53	Wife of Tailor (Welsh)
8	25th ,,	27th August	1, Miles' court, Cae-draw	F.	50	Wife of Hawker (Scotch)
9	26th ,,	30th ,,	8, Coffin's ct., George Town	F.	80	Wife of Skinner (Welsh)
10	27th ,,	1st September	4, Lewis' square, Abercannaid	F.	32	Wife of Collier (Welsh)
11	28th ,,	1st ,,	9, Sunny Bank	F.	42	Wife of Labourer (Irish)
12	3rd September	5th ,, }	13, Mt. Pleasant, {	F.	21	{ Wife and } of
13	6th ,,	8th ,, }	Penydarren {	F.	8	{ Daughter } Collier (Welsh)

66

Cholera in Epidemic of 1866, in Merthyr Tydfil.

Circumstances.	Habits.	Any evidence of contagion or infection.	State of the Dwellings or Neighbourhood.
Very poor	Dirty	No possible contact	Damp, dirty, and unventilated.
Poor	Dirty	ditto	Dirty, unventilated—yard at back most filthy.
Good	Clean and regular	ditto	A drain, which carries away house slops from houses above, runs under the house.
Poor	Clean	As a rag cleaner might have picked infected clothes	An untrapped gully at end of court, also heaps of ashes steeped with excrement, &c. House, no ventilation.
Young Irish Labourer	Regular	No possible contact	Cesspool at back of house above level of lower floor—offensive.
Very poor	Dirty	ditto	Court unpaved, no convenience, earth sodden with house refuse.
Very poor	Intemperate & Dirty	ditto	Cesspool in garden overflowing, floor of sleeping room thickly covered with dirt and filth.
Poor	Clean and regular	Her husband and herself travelled about the neighbouring towns—had been in Aberdare	Cesspool near house overflowing.
Poor	Very clean	Had attended her son, case No. 3	Unventilated—common cesspool in gardens full.
Comfortable	Clean and regular	Apparently spontaneous	Overcrowded with family and lodgers—9 out of the 12 attacked, 7 died. At back of bedroom heap of ashes foul with excrement.
Comfortable	Clean	May have visited case No. 7	
Comfortable	Clean	No known contact	{Unceiled cow shed under the house in a most filthy state.

o'clock and sometimes later. We get 2p a day and our light costs us 2½p a week. Rachel was in a day school and she can read a little. She was run over by a tram a while ago and was home ill a long time, but she has got over it'.

Girls and boys like these helped to raise 1500 tons of coal each day, all of which was used by the same iron works.

The mines in the Llanelli area were about 500 feet deep. Many of these had ladders fixed to the walls of the shafts with platforms every 20 or 30 yards. The youngest boys were five and six years old and were carried down the mines on the backs of their fathers or friends. Coming up they were generally put in the baskets which were used to raise coal. These baskets were operated by steam engines. There were no records of young girls working in these pits.

Phillip Philip was ten years of age and worked at the Brace colliery as a carter. *'I help my brother to cart. I can go down the ladders by myself. I am not afraid to go down the pit'.*

The inspector climbed down these ladders and said he found difficulty in doing so. He was also afraid of the noise and the heavy rods of the pump engine so close to the ladders.

Descending a mine today can be a smooth and fast journey in a modern cage. Dangers still exist in the mining industry and perhaps will always be present, unfortunately, but conditions have altered out of recognition since the last century with its countless miseries and hardships for those involved in obtaining coal.

Glossary of Terms:

Many of the terms defined here were in common use throughout the mining industry but some were used only locally.

Bait: food taken to work.

Baisted: punished by being hit as in 'I was baisted.' In South Wales the word became 'pasted' as in 'I'll give you a pasting'.

Barrow-way: very narrow low passages between the coalface and the rolley-ways.

By or bye: as in 'far in by' meaning 'far into the pit'; opposite 'out by' meaning towards the shaft.

Fired a little: small explosion of gas in the pit.

Foal: child who pulled a tram.

Galloways: horse that pulled the rolleys.

Gob: the area where coal has been mined and filled in afterwards with waste material.

Corf: plural corves. A wicker basket for containing coal. Could hold 4 to 7 cwt. Made of hazel rods half to one inch in diameter. Sometimes used to raise or lower workers in the shaft.

Headsman: person who pulled a tram, older than a foal.

Half-marrow: child who pulled or pushed a tram.

Hammers: as in 'I got my hammers' meaning 'I was beaten.'

Horse-way: the main passages where horses could be used for hauling.

Hurrier:	name given to a person who hauled the coal sometimes paid according to the distance 'hurried'.
Jinny-boys:	operated the pulley system when coal was hauled up inclines or slopes.
Level:	a tunnel into sloping ground similar to a cave. The coal was then mined without having to dig.a shaft. Very common in hilly areas.
Loose:	a term which was shouted by groups of workers in turn to signify the end of the shift.
Putters:	a general term for those who handled the trams between the coalface and the rolley ways.
Rolleys:	wagons used in the large passages leading to the pit bottom. In the north east they were about 7 foot 6 inches long and could hold three corves. Usually drawn by horses.
Staith:	high wooden structure from which the coal was unloaded from the wagons into the holds of ships.
Singin hinni:	a rich cake; so called from the singing noise it emits as it cooks.
Skip:	a platform on which workers or coal were raised or lowered in a shaft by means of a horse gin.
Strap:	to hit as in 'He gave me a strapping'.
Toom:	or tume, meaning empty as in 'The tume corf'.

Trapper: one who sat and opened and closed a ventilation door when coal passed through.

Tue: to fatigue or chafe as in 'I was sore tued a heaving' meaning 'I was tired and raw after heaving the coal'.

Yard wand: a stick used to measure the length of coal cut or a distance it had to be hauled. The stick was often used to punish children.

Printed by Estate Printers Ltd., Treforest Industrial Estate, Pontypridd
Mid. Glamorgan CF37 5UF